Continue Your Journey

with Thrive

Book 7 in the Internet Marketing FAST series

Copyright and Enquiries

Comments or enquiries may be left in the *Contact Me* page at:

https://superaffiliatechallenge.com/contact-me/

Book 7 in the Internet Marketing FAST series

Continue Your Journey

with Thrive

Contents

Continue Your Journey

with Thrive

Continue Your Journey

with Thrive

Continue Your Journey

with Thrive

Table of Figures

Continue Your Journey

with Thrive

Continue Your Journey

with Thrive

Continue Your Journey

with Thrive

Continue Your Journey

with Thrive

The Essential Thrive

The previous book in this series, *Building Your Website with Thrive Themes and Plugins*, covers getting Thrive Themes and Plugins, installing the Product Manager plugin, installing a theme and some plugins, customizing your WordPress website and basic use of Thrive Architect, Thrive's drag and drop page editor.

To purchase Thrive Themes or simply to investigate further, please click:

<u>THRIVE THEMES AND PLUGINS</u>

The previous book covered these Thrive Architect elements and their usage.

- Text (used for a heading)
- Text (used for a paragraph)
- Image
- Content Box
- Inserting a Link
- Wrapping text around an image
- The More tag
- Post Grid

This user guide covers the rest.

Continue Your Journey

with Thrive

Thrive Architect: Drag and Drop Elements

An element is simply an item, such as text or an image, that you can drag and drop to its desired position on your page or blog post.

When you want to edit an element, you can just click on it to see its properties in the options panel to the left of the screen.

Some elements are quite complex, with for example a button and a text box inside a column inside a column group inside a content box.

Often, the easiest way is to check the breadcrumb trail at the top of the screen and select which part of the element you want to edit there.

Figure 1: Follow the Breadcrumbs

Continue Your Journey
with Thrive

The Elements

Button

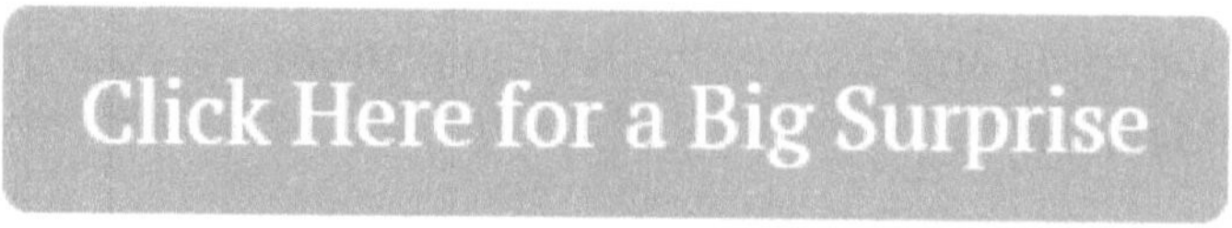

Figure 2: Button Element

The button element allows you to add a button to your page. You control the size, the shape, the color, the text and what happens when the button is clicked or pressed.

Columns

As the name implies, the Columns element allows you to divide a section of your page into columns for the purpose of displaying other elements, such as text and images, side by side.

Continue Your Journey

with Thrive

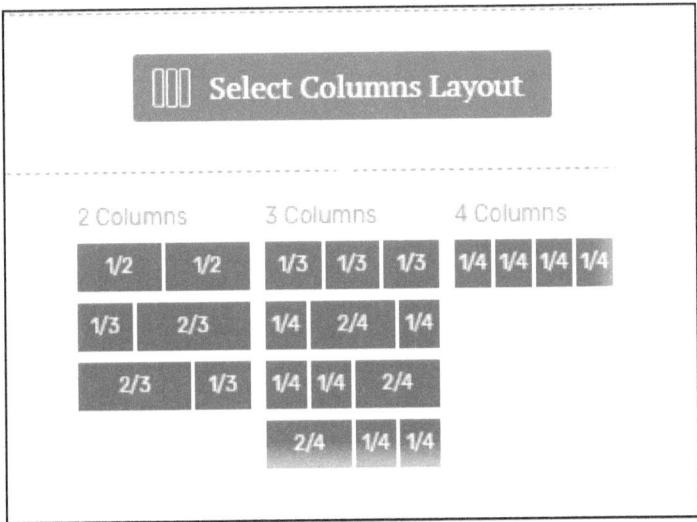

Figure 3: Select Columns Layout

You can select a 2, 3 or 4 column layout, with variations within each.

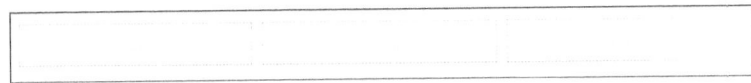

Figure 4: Three Column Layout

A 3-column layout has been selected, ready to accept elements.

Continue Your Journey

with Thrive

Figure 5: Putting Stuff Inside Columns

In this example, I've put an image into column 1 and right-aligned it, some text into column 2 and another set of columns into column 3.

You can get some great effects with the smart use of columns.

Background Section

After the page itself, a background section is the largest container on the page and can be used for dramatic effects, including full-screen color gradient, image or video.

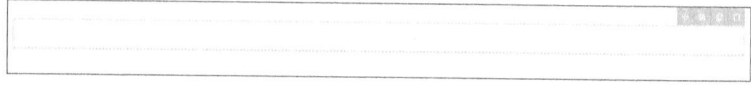

Figure 6: Initial Background Section

It starts off as an innocuous rectangle.

Go to the Options menu on the left to see some of the effects you can have.

As an example, I'm going to cover the whole screen with a background image.

Continue Your Journey

with Thrive

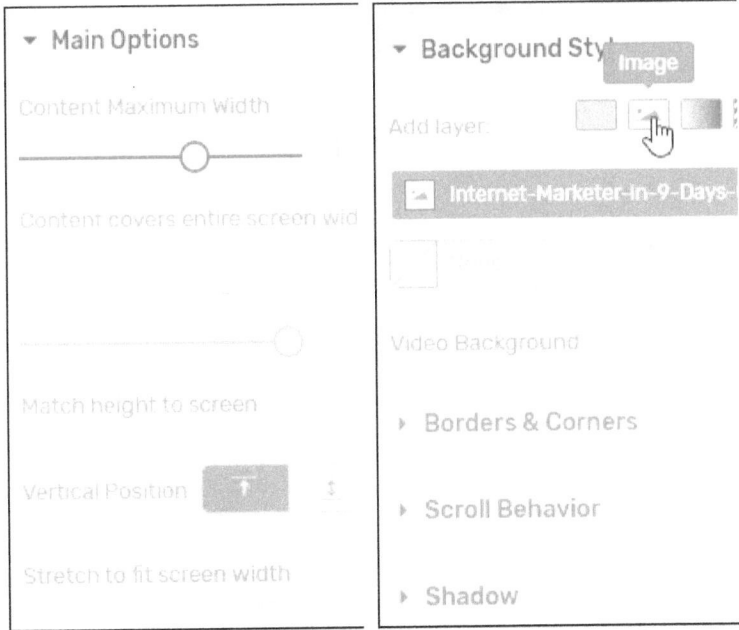

Figure 7: Main Options Set to Cover Screen

Figure 8: Background Style Set to Image

which looks like this on a smart phone:

Continue Your Journey
with Thrive

Figure 9: Full Screen Background

Other elements can then be placed inside the background section.

Continue Your Journey

with Thrive

Templates & Symbols

Templates and Symbols allow you to save an element (or a group of elements) so that they can be re-used on other pages.

The difference between the two is that Symbols are globally synchronized and Templates are not.

You could insert a Template on 10 different pages and make changes on one or more pages without affecting the others.

If the content was a Symbol, however, making a change on any one page would automatically make the same change on the other 9 pages.

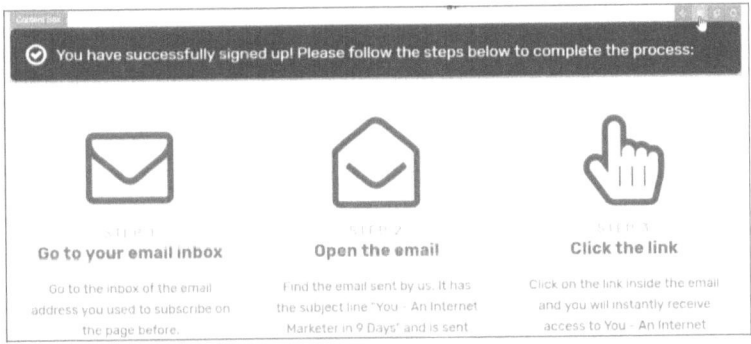

Figure 10: Save Content Box

Here I've selected a Content Box (and the elements inside it) so as to be able to reuse it elsewhere.

Continue Your Journey

with Thrive

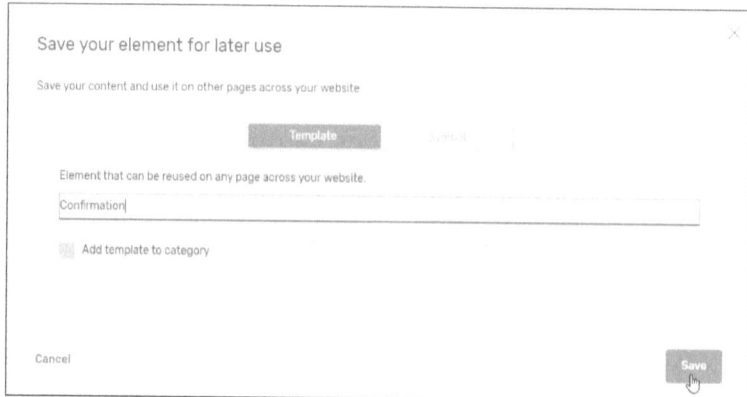

Figure 11: Save Content Box as Template

You can save the element as a Template or a Symbol and if you have a lot of them, you can group them into Categories.

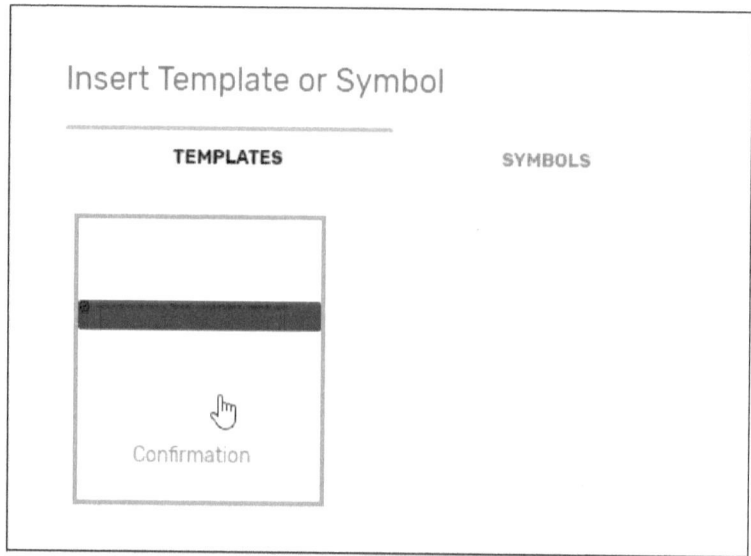

Figure 12: Select the Saved Template

Continue Your Journey

with Thrive

Then, when you select the Templates and Symbols element, you will be able to choose from your saved templates and symbols to have it automatically inserted on the page.

Click to Tweet

This allows you to display a tweet and invite your visitor to share it with their Twitter followers.

By default, it will point back to this post, but you can change that if you wish.

Figure 13: Click to Tweet

Continue Your Journey

with Thrive

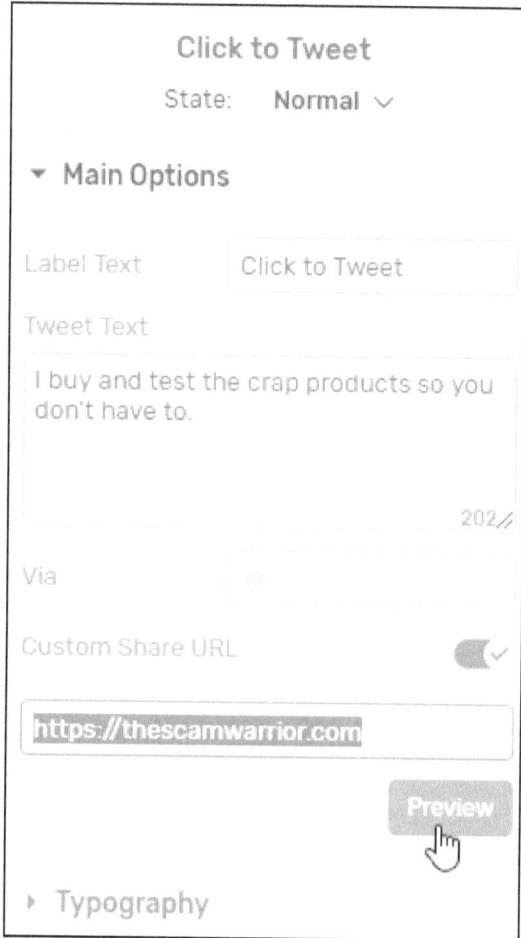

Figure 14: Click to Tweet Main Options

Continue Your Journey

with Thrive

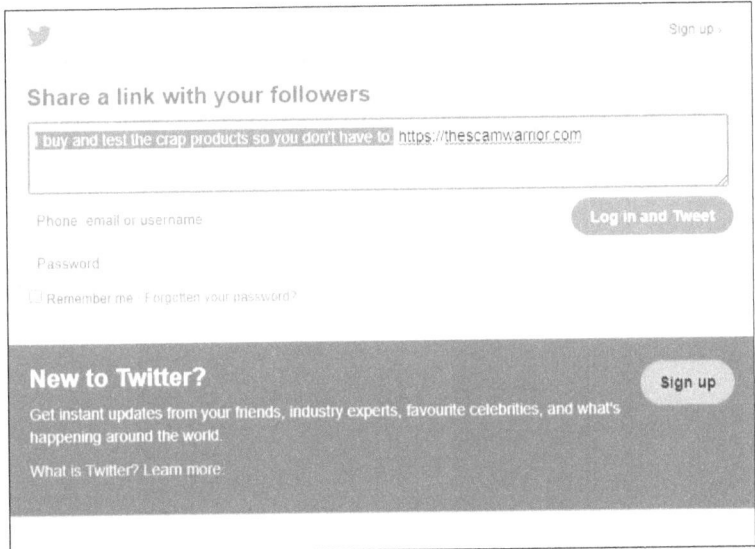

Figure 15: Click to Tweet Preview

Content Reveal

The Content Reveal element allows you to put other elements inside the Content Reveal box and display them only after a specified time has elapsed.

So you might have a special announcement that's not visible when the visitor first opens the page or post, but which appears, say, 5 seconds later.

If the Content Reveal box is below the fold, you can choose an option to automatically scroll down to it.

Continue Your Journey

with Thrive

Use this with caution. It's very annoying to be reading something on a page or post and then have it suddenly disappear as the screen auto-scrolls down.

You can also redirect to a different URL as soon as the Content Reveal appears.

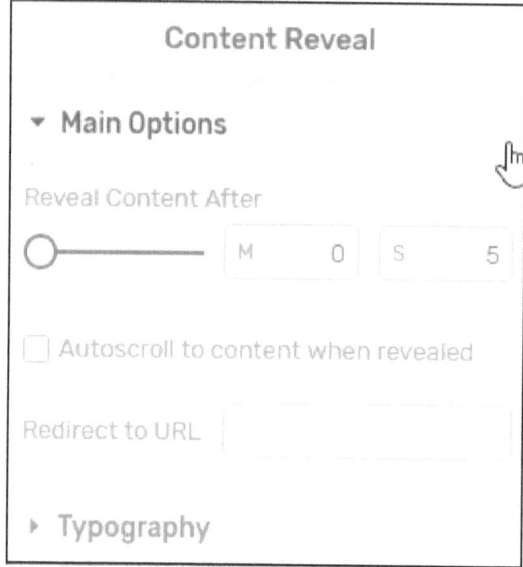

Figure 16: Content Reveal Options

Countdown

A countdown timer allows you to add a scarcity factor to an offer.

Continue Your Journey

with Thrive

Figure 17: Countdown Main Options

You can set the Style, such as Rounded, the color, the end date, the current time, the Timezone and the message to show when the countdown reaches zero.

I believe that it's important that the countdown be genuine. I've seen sites where the counter

Continue Your Journey

with Thrive

restarts each time you enter the site. So it's false scarcity. I abandon such sites immediately as not having integrity.

Continue Your Journey

with Thrive

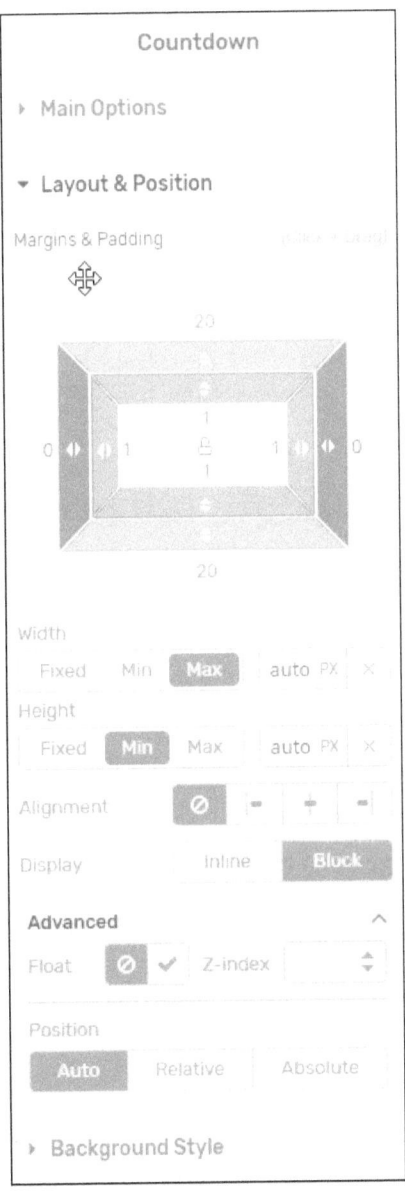

Figure 18: Countdown Layout and Position Options

25

Continue Your Journey

The Countdown Layout and Position Options allow you to specify such things as size and alignment, as well as being able to float text around it.

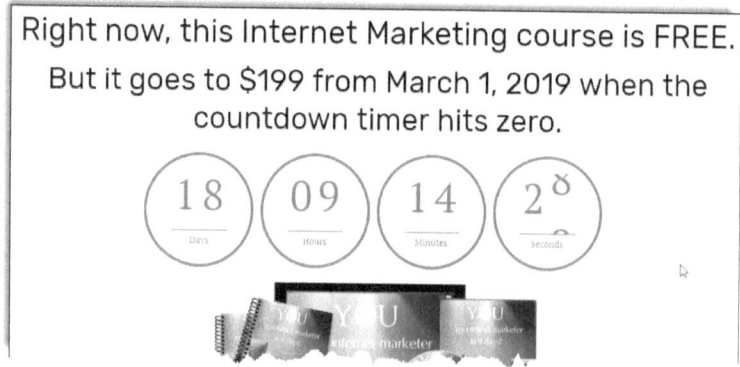

Figure 19: Countdown Timer in Action

Countdown Evergreen

The Countdown Evergreen element is almost identical to the Countdown element, but adds an option to restart the countdown after a specified elapsed time.

Credit Card

With the Credit Card element, you can choose which credit cards you take as payment and display their icons as a banner.

Continue Your Journey

with Thrive

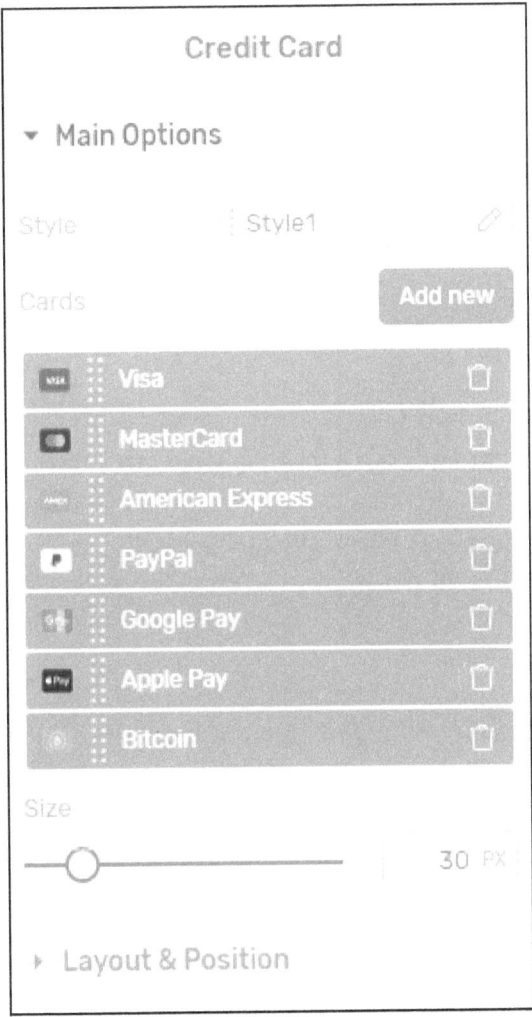

Figure 20: Credit Card Element Options

This would result in the following image displayed on your page.

Continue Your Journey

with Thrive

Figure 21: Credit Card Display

Custom HTML

Occasionally, you will need to put some html (hyper text markup language) code onto a page to interface with a third-party platform such as an autoresponder or a payment gateway like PayPal. They will provide the html code and this is how you'll insert it.

Custom Menu

The Custom Menu element allows you to display a menu on your page. The menu can be based on an existing, pre-defined menu or you can create a totally new one.

Disqus Comments

Disqus is a third-party application for getting comment engagement and handling moderation. You can learn and join up at https://disqus.com/.

The Disqus element puts the discussion topic right there on your page for your visitors to engage.

Continue Your Journey

with Thrive

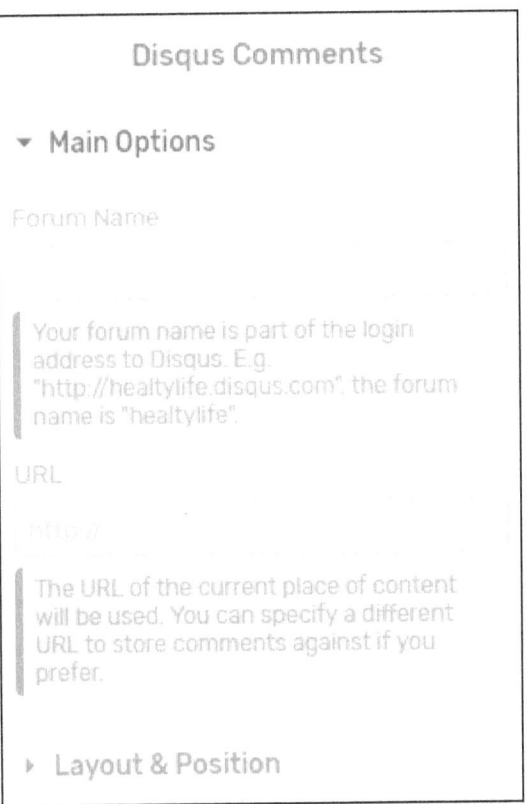

Figure 22: Disqus Main Options

You need to enter your Disqus Forum Name and the URL for comment storage.

The Disqus panel is displayed on your page or blog post, ready to interact with your visitors.

Continue Your Journey

with Thrive

Figure 23: Disqus Panel

Divider

Use the Divider element for a simple straight-line divider to separate one section from another.

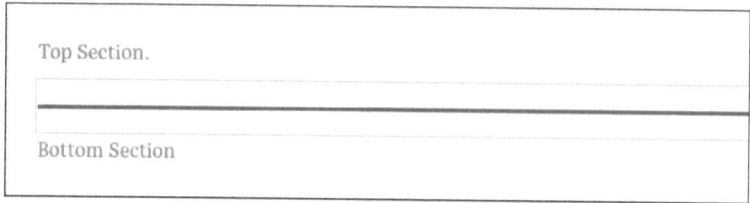

Figure 24: Divider Between Two Text Elements

You can control the style, color, thickness and position of the divider.

Continue Your Journey
with Thrive

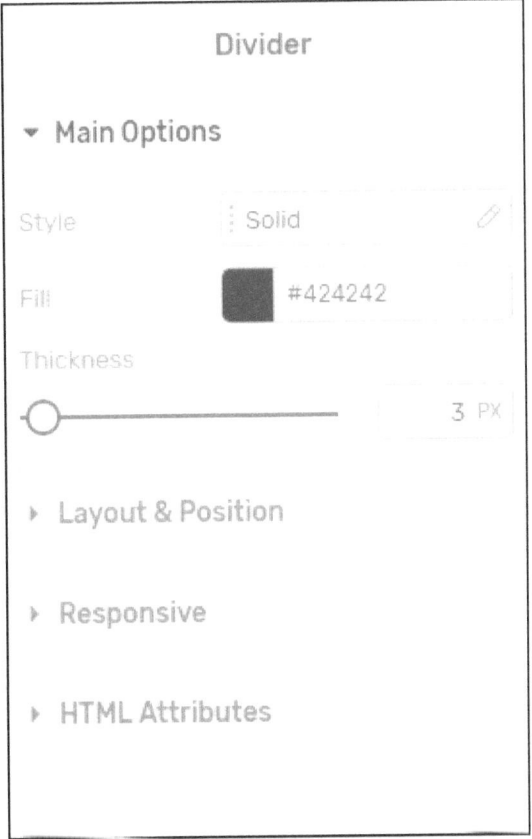

Figure 25: Divider Options

Facebook Comments

The Facebook Comments element allows moderated Facebook comments on your post or page.

Continue Your Journey

with Thrive

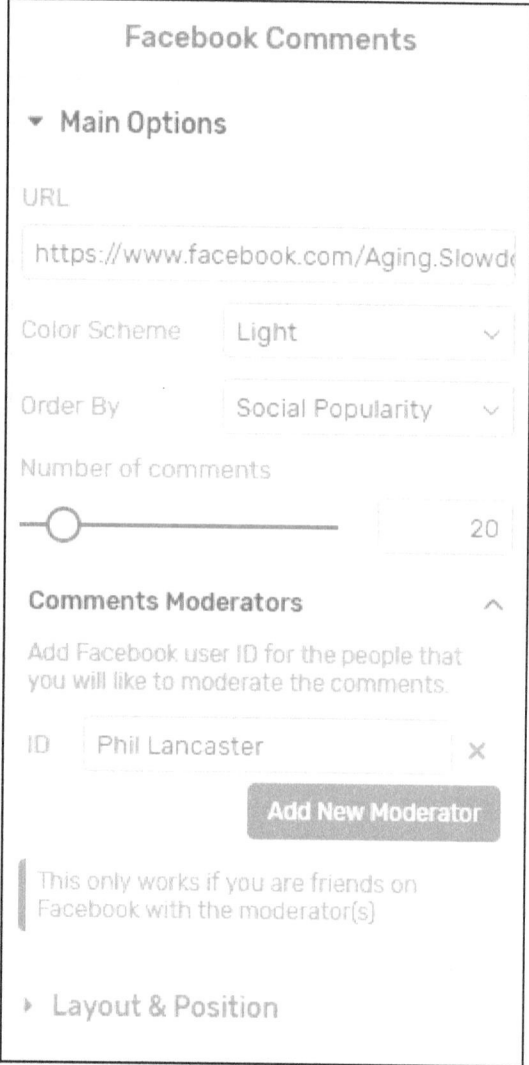

Figure 26: Facebook Comments Options

You enter the URL of your Facebook page and your Facebook user ID so that you can moderate comments.

Continue Your Journey

with Thrive

Alternatively, you can nominate a Facebook friend as a moderator. You can have more than one moderator.

You can also specify the maximum number of Facebook comments to be displayed on the post or page.

Figure 27: Facebook Comments Directly on Post or Page

Your visitors can post Facebook style comments directly into the panel and optionally post them to your Facebook page as well.

Continue Your Journey

with Thrive

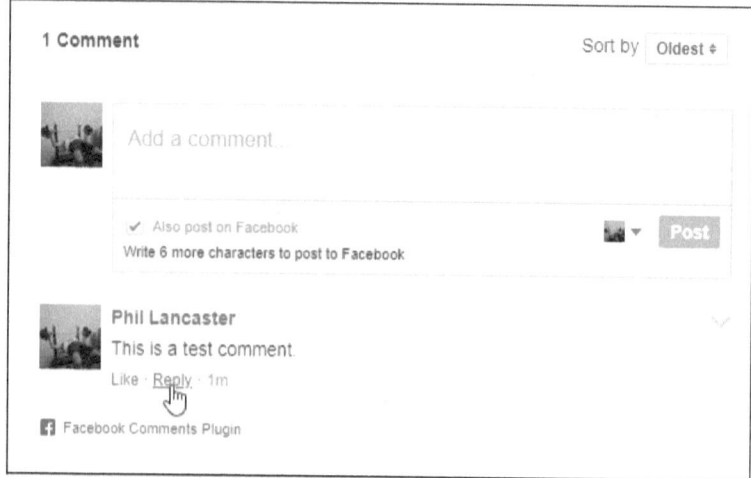

Figure 28: A Comment Has Been Added

The comment is shown on the post or page and can be liked or replied to by other visitors.

Fill Counter

This is just a simple display that you can put on a page to show the visitor that they are part way through a process

Continue Your Journey

with Thrive

Figure 29: Fill Counter Set to 75%

You can control size, color, position and what percentage to show.

Continue Your Journey

with Thrive

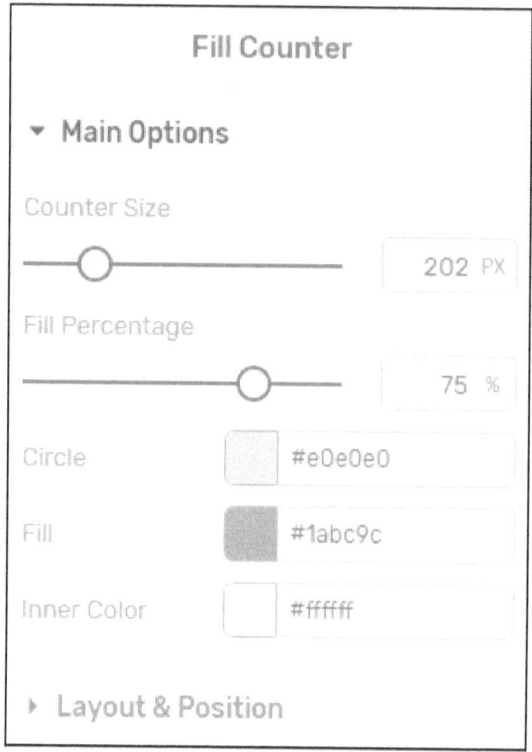

Figure 30: Fill Counter Options

For an alternative way of displaying the same thing, see Progress Bar on page 47.

Google Map

The Google Map element puts an interactive Google Map into your page or post.

Continue Your Journey

with Thrive

Figure 31: Interactive Google Map

By default, the map is full screen width. To control its size and position, put it inside a Content Box.

Continue Your Journey

with Thrive

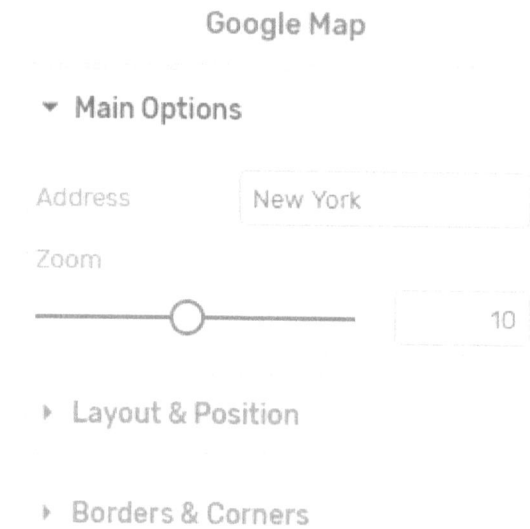

Figure 32: Specify the Map's Location and Initial Zoom

In the Options section, you can specify what part of the world you want to display and the initial zoom factor.

Icon

Simply allows you to choose from a large database of icons.

Continue Your Journey

with Thrive

Figure 33: Choose an Icon

Here's an example.

Figure 34: The Bitcoin Icon Selected

You can control its properties in the usual way.

Continue Your Journey

with Thrive

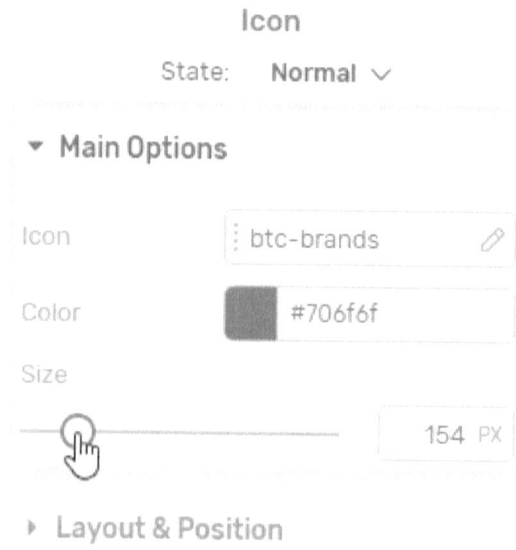

Figure 35: Set the Icon's Properties

Lead Generation

The purpose of the Lead Generation element is to capture your visitor's name and email address into your autoresponder.

Before you can use the Lead Generation element, you must connect your website to your auto responder as described in Lesson 4: Part 1 under

Thrive Themes

 Customizations

  Autoresponder

Continue Your Journey

with Thrive

Then you can select the autoresponder connection for the Lead Generation.

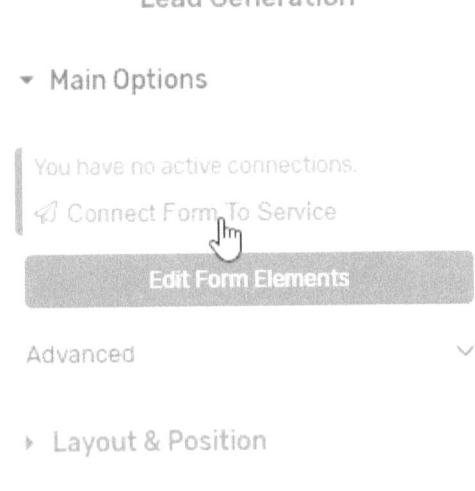

Figure 36: Click on Connect Form to Service

Then select the autoresponder to connect to.

Continue Your Journey

with Thrive

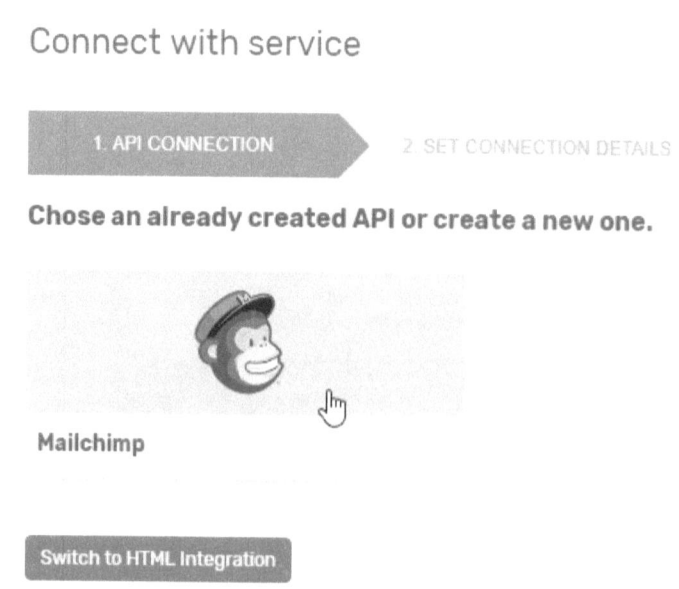

Figure 37: Connect to MailChimp

Then you can select which list to connect to, if you have more than one and, if appropriate, which group within that list.

Continue Your Journey

with Thrive

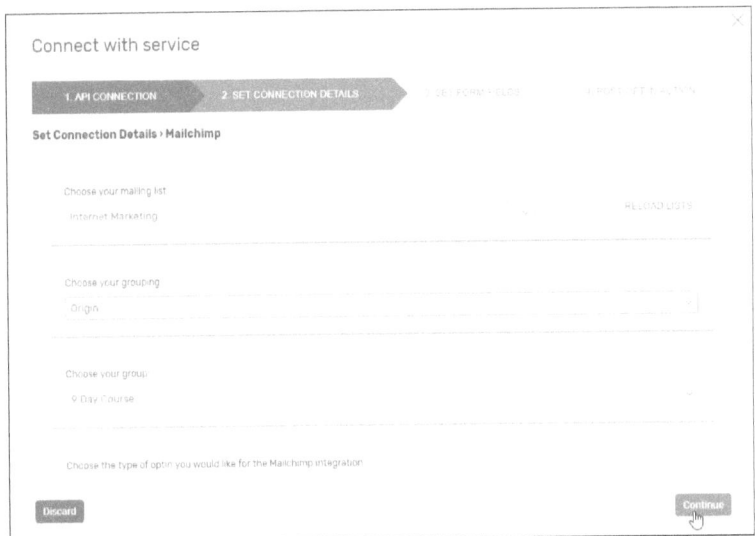

Figure 38: Select the Mailing List and Group

Specify which fields are to appear on the form and whether or not they are required.

Figure 39: Specify the Fields to Appear on the Form

Continue Your Journey

with Thrive

Finally, decide what action is to be taken after your visitor successfully completes the form.

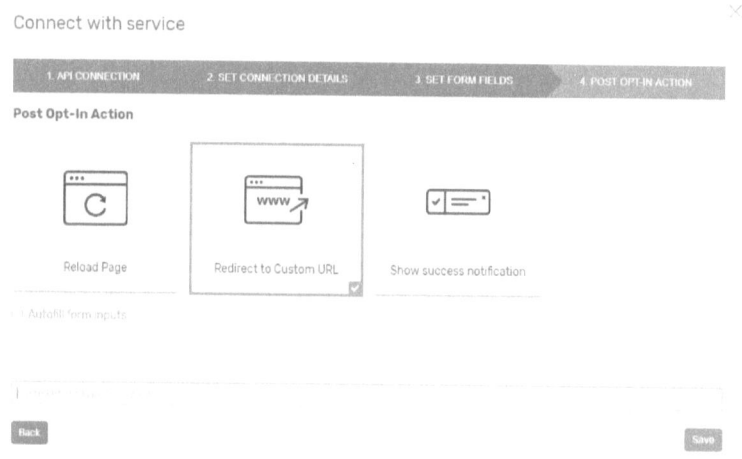

Figure 40: Decide Post Opt-in Action

You can select between Reload Page, Redirect to Custom URL and Show Success Notification.

Usually, you want to direct them to a thank you page that tells them to click on a link in the email that's been sent to them to take them to the next stage (probably a download).

Lead Generation is covered in Lesson 7: Opt-in Offers and Autoresponder.

Continue Your Journey

with Thrive

Figure 41: Opt-in Form

The lead generation (opt-in) form then appears on your post or page. To control its size and position, put it inside a Content Box.

You can also control the appearance of the elements inside the form.

Continue Your Journey

with Thrive

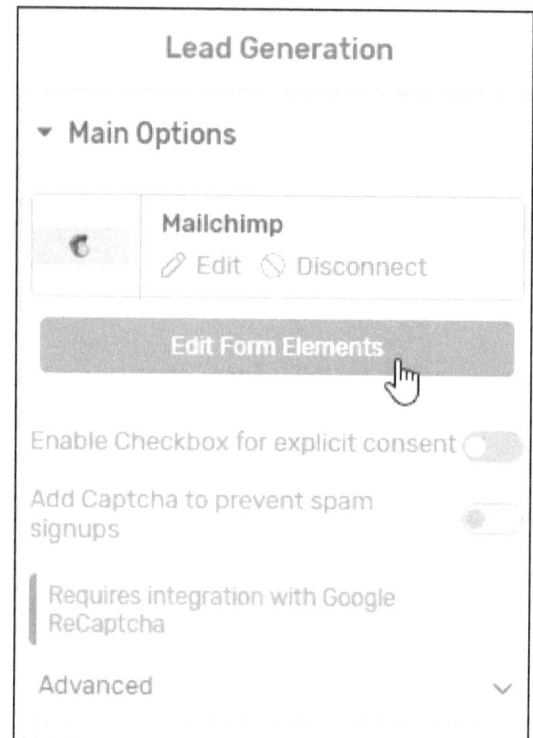

Figure 42: Edit the Opt-in Form Elements

Figure 43: Opt-in Form Ready to Use

Here's the same form with the button reduced 50%, its color changed and an icon added.

Continue Your Journey

with Thrive

Progress Bar

This is just a simple display that you can put on a page to show the visitor that they are part way through a process

Figure 44: Progress Bar

You can control size, color, font, position and what percentage to show.

Continue Your Journey

with Thrive

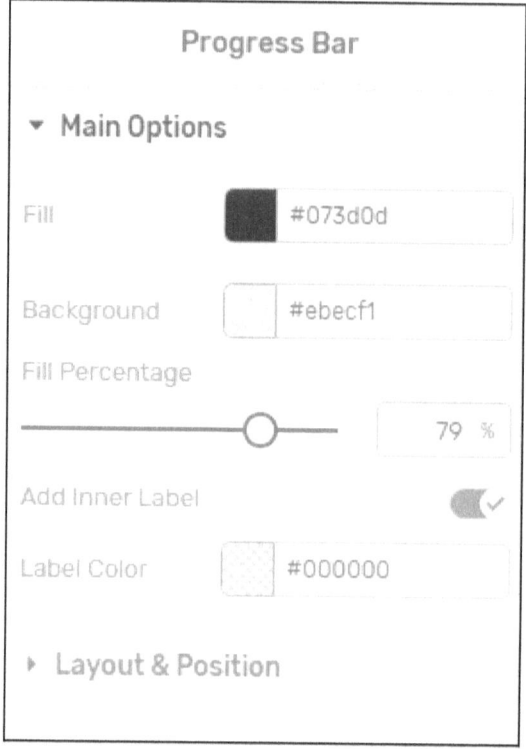

Figure 45: Progress Bar Options

For an alternative way of displaying the same thing, see Fill Counter on page 34.

Social Share

The Social Share element invites your visitors to share your post or page on their social media.

Continue Your Journey

with Thrive

Figure 46: Invite Your Visitor to Share

You control which social media platforms are displayed and the size and format of the display.

You can also specify a different URL as the one to be shared.

Continue Your Journey

with Thrive

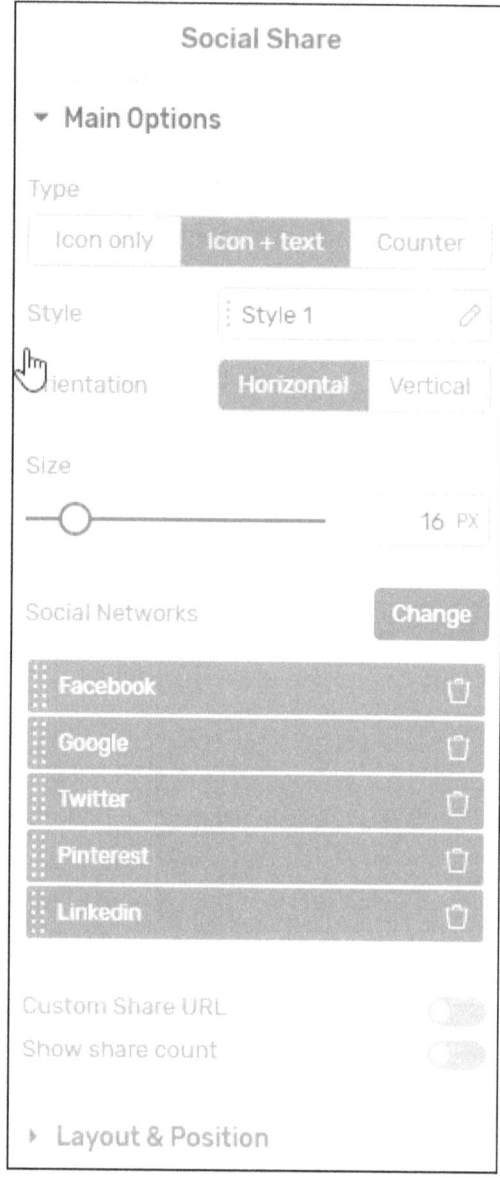

Figure 47: Social Share Options

Continue Your Journey

Global Social Share Icons

You can also control the appearance of social media icons in Thrive Dashboard >> Theme Options >> Social Media.

Here, you can cause the social media icons to display at the side of every post and/or every page and optionally float them so that they stay in position as the post or page is scrolled.

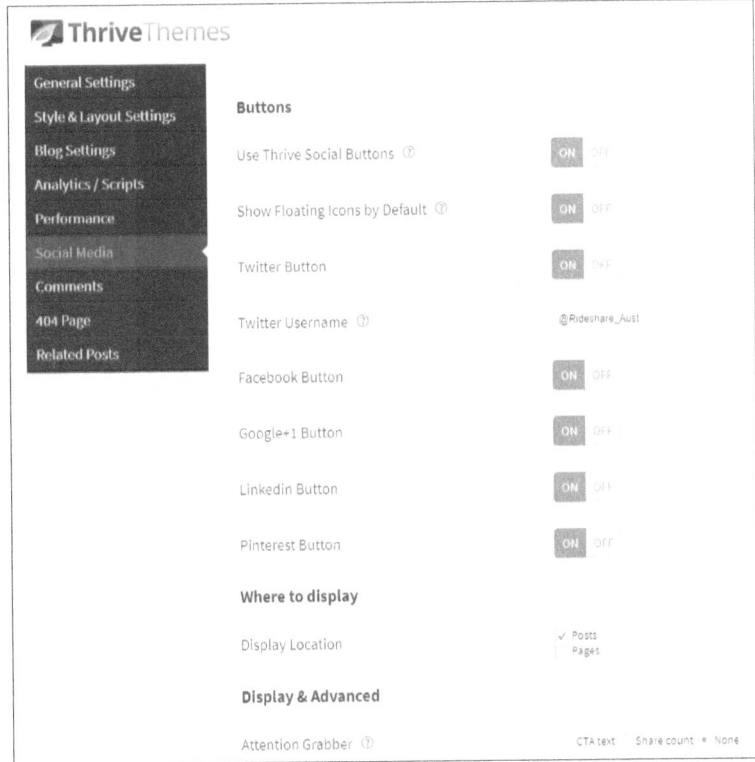

Figure 48: Social Media in Theme Options

51

Continue Your Journey

These settings would result in the social media icons for Twitter, Facebook, Google+, Linkedin and Pinterest to float beside every post.

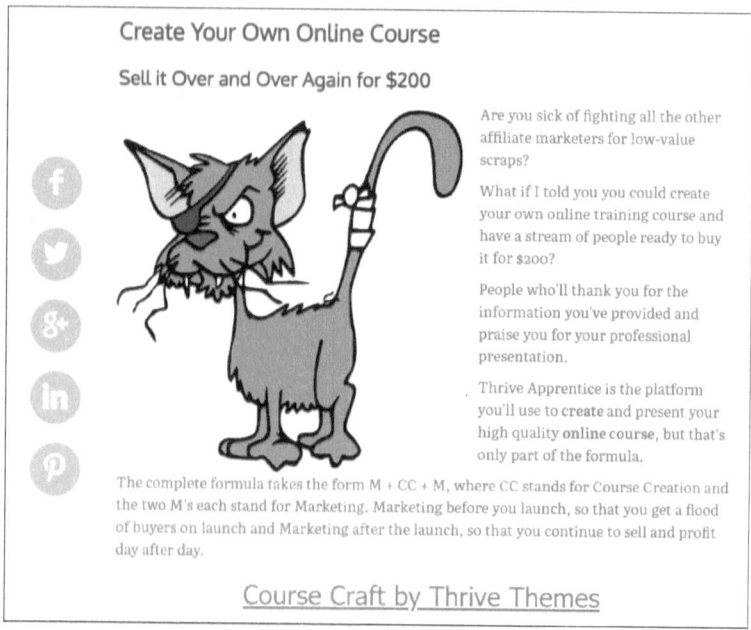

Create Your Own Online Course

Sell it Over and Over Again for $200

Are you sick of fighting all the other affiliate marketers for low-value scraps?

What if I told you you could create your own online training course and have a stream of people ready to buy it for $200?

People who'll thank you for the information you've provided and praise you for your professional presentation.

Thrive Apprentice is the platform you'll use to **create** and present your high quality **online course**, but that's only part of the formula.

The complete formula takes the form M + CC + M, where CC stands for Course Creation and the two M's each stand for Marketing. Marketing before you launch, so that you get a flood of buyers on launch and Marketing after the launch, so that you continue to sell and profit day after day.

Course Craft by Thrive Themes

Figure 49: Blog Post with Floating Social Media Icons

Note that you can set this up but then activate or deactivate it just by setting the first option on or off.

Star Rating

The Star Rating element provides a visual star rating. Very useful for review sites.

Continue Your Journey

with Thrive

Figure 50: Three and a Half Star Rating

You can control all aspects of how the rating appears.

Continue Your Journey

with Thrive

Figure 51: Star Rating Options

You control size, style, colors and of course how many stars and half stars are awarded.

Styled List

The Styled List element shows a list on your post or page, where you control just how the list should look. It's a more sophisticated version of the standard bullet point list.

Continue Your Journey

with Thrive

- ✔ List Element

- ✔ List Element

- ✔ List Element

Figure 52: Styled List Default

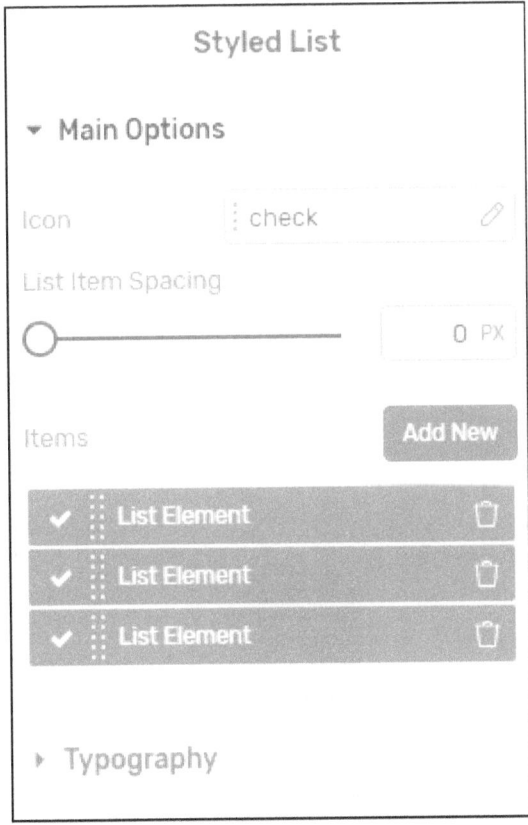

Figure 53: Styled List Options

Continue Your Journey

with Thrive

Here's the same list with some options updated to get the look I wanted.

4 Key Advantages of Thrive Themes

🔑 **Conversion Optimized Themes**

🔑 **Drag and Drop Editor**

🔑 **Automated Split Testing**

🔑 **Online Course Creation**

Figure 54: Modified Styled List

Table

The table element allows you to insert a table into the post or page and then control its contents and appearance.

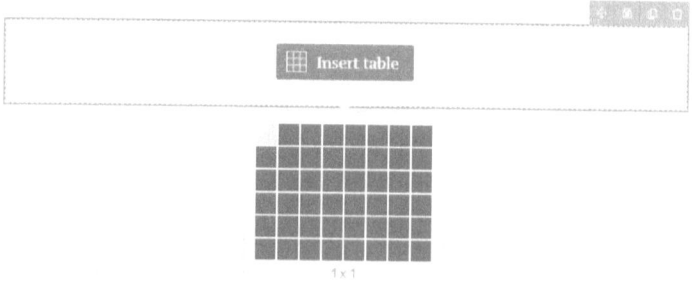

Figure 55: Specify the Number of Rows and Columns

Start off by specifying the number of rows and columns.

Continue Your Journey

Let's create a table with 4 rows and 3 columns.

Figure 56: Empty 4-Row 3-Column Table

Notice that the first row has automatically been designated as a header row. This allows you to give it different characteristics from the content rows.

Continue Your Journey

with Thrive

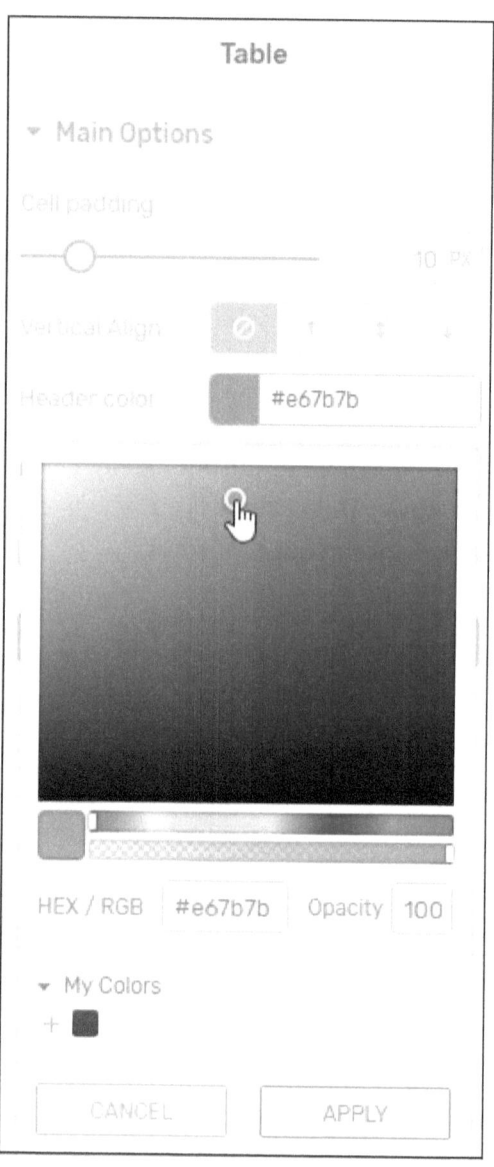

Figure 57: Giving the Header Row a Different Color

Continue Your Journey

This results in

Figure 58: Header Row New Color

Click on *Manage Cells* in Table Properties to add and delete rows and columns or to split and merge cells.

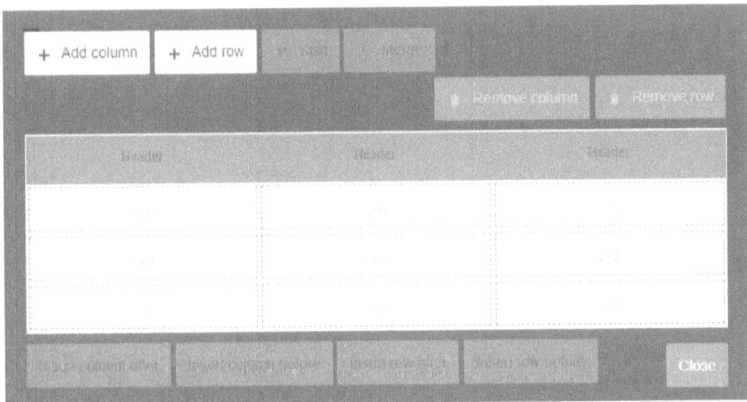

Figure 59: Manage Table Cells

From there, it's just a matter of adding the content you want to the table by dragging and dropping the elements you want, such as Text and Images.

Continue Your Journey

Figure 60: Table with Some Content Added

Finally, you can specify the table borders that you want (or none at all, if you just want the controlled positioning that a table can give you).

Continue Your Journey

with Thrive

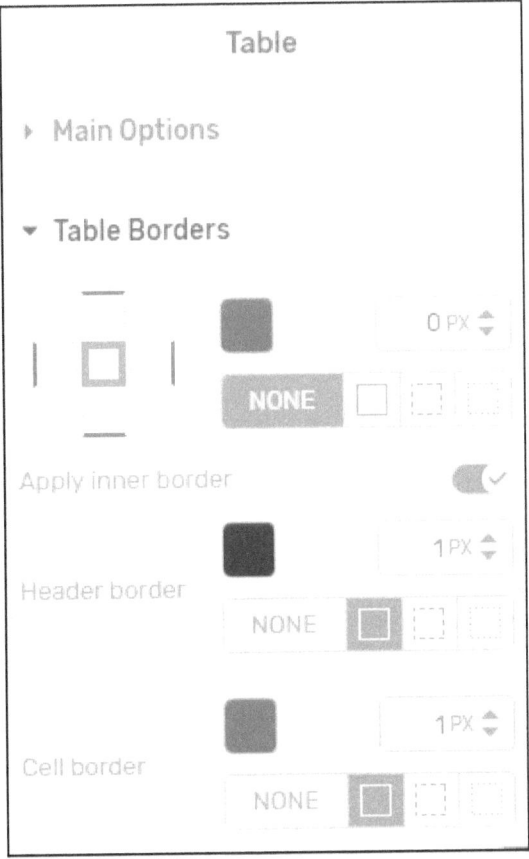

Figure 61: Specify Table Borders

Table of Contents

The Table of Contents element puts a table of contents into your post or page to give your visitor quick navigation within the post or page.

Continue Your Journey

with Thrive

You specify what heading levels are to be used.

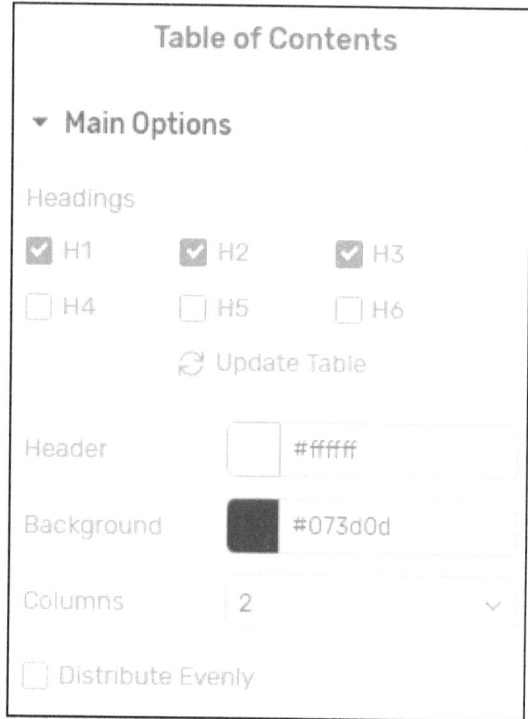

Figure 62: Set Heading Levels for TOC

This gives a Table of Contents like this:

Continue Your Journey

with Thrive

Create Online Course

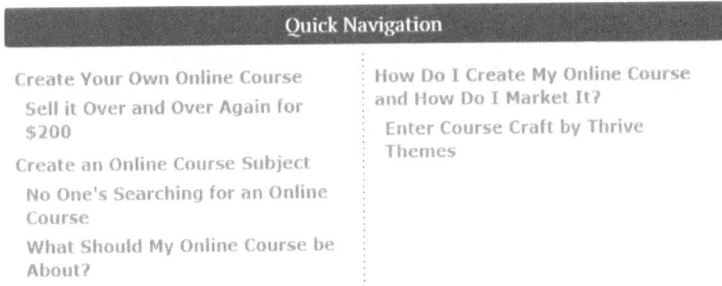

Figure 63: Table of Contents

Tabs

The Tabs element allows you to put information inside tabs on your post or page, so that the information is revealed only when the visitor clicks on the tab.

This can be a great way of making a long post more accessible. Instead of having, say, three related paragraphs one after the other, put them in three tabs, occupying the same screen space.

This also encourages interaction from your visitor.

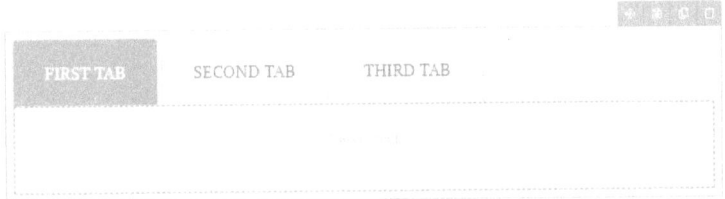

Figure 64: The Tabs Element

Continue Your Journey

You control the tabs options, including number of labs, the layout, the color and, of course, the content.

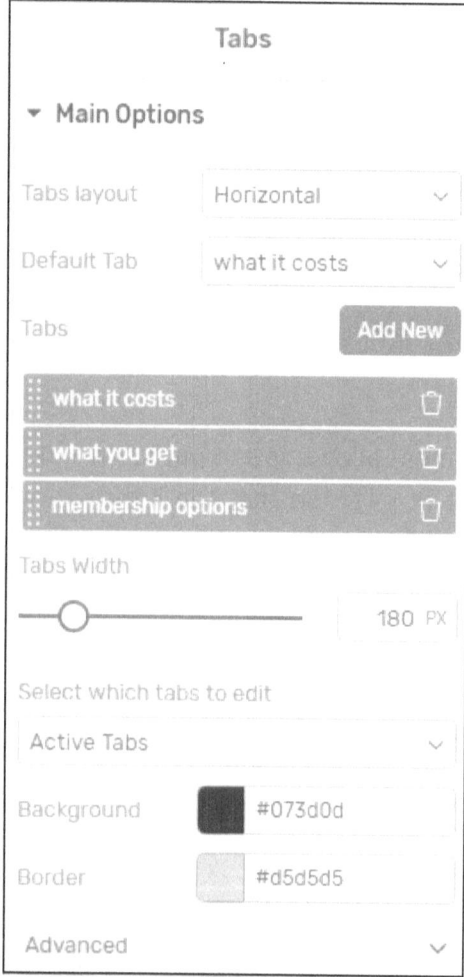

Figure 65: Tabs Options

Here, three paragraphs that originally came one after the other, making a very long blog entry, have been moved into

Continue Your Journey

three tabs, giving the visitor more control over the reading experience.

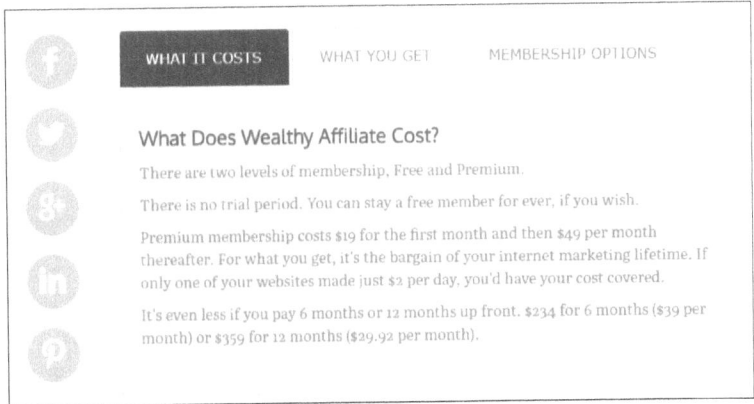

Figure 66: Three Tabs with Content

Testimonial

There's no doubt that good, genuine testimonials help to sell product. But the presentation of the testimonial is a factor as well. The Testimonial element allows you to choose from a wide variety of testimonial templates. If you can get your reviewers to submit photographs, always choose a template that uses them.

Continue Your Journey

with Thrive

Figure 67: Choose Testimonial Template

Best part of the testimonials goes here...

Display testimonials here and make them more skimmable by adding a teaser or the best part from the testimonial as a headline. A good testimonial can make all the difference to your conversion rates.

DANA MOORE // Designer

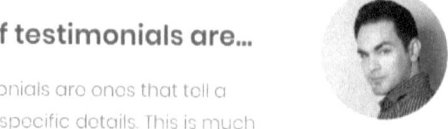

The best kinds of testimonials are...

The best kinds of testimonials are ones that tell a small story and include specific details. This is much more powerful than a generic testimonial that simply say "I love this product!" or something similarly vague.

MARC JACOBS // Business Analyst

Figure 68: Complete the Template Details

Continue Your Journey

Then it's just a matter of substituting the text and images to create your attractive and professional looking testimonials.

Toggle

The toggle element allows you to create content that is revealed to the visitor only after they click on the toggle heading.

This can help to make the user feel special. It's a "click here to reveal secret stuff" type of thing.

It starts off pretty simple.

Figure 69: Change the Toggle Headline

Change the Content Toggle Headline and then insert the elements to be revealed.

Figure 70: Change the Heading and Add Your Content

You can add any sort of content, including text and images, that will be revealed when your visitor clicks on your toggle heading.

Continue Your Journey

▾ Congratulations! You have been selected to receive free training.

Are you sick of fighting all the other affiliate marketers for low-value scraps?

What if I told you you could create your own online training course and have a stream of people ready to buy it for $200?

People who'll thank you for the information you've provided and praise you for your professional presentation.

Thrive Apprentice is the platform you'll use to **create** and present your high quality **online course**, but that's only part of the formula.

The complete formula takes the form M + CC + M, where CC stands for Course Creation and the two M's each stand for Marketing. Marketing before you launch, so that you get a flood of buyers on launch and Marketing after the launch, so that you continue to sell and profit day after day.

Figure 71: After Adding Some Detail

And this is what it looks like on your post or page.

▸ Congratulations! You have been selected to receive free training.

Figure 72: The Toggle as it Appears

And when your visitor clicks on it, they get the information you've added.

Video

Video is really simple. It allows you to insert a video on your post or page from a variety of sources. These include

Continue Your Journey

with Thrive

- YouTube
- Vimeo
- Wistia
- Anywhere else, including your own hard disk.

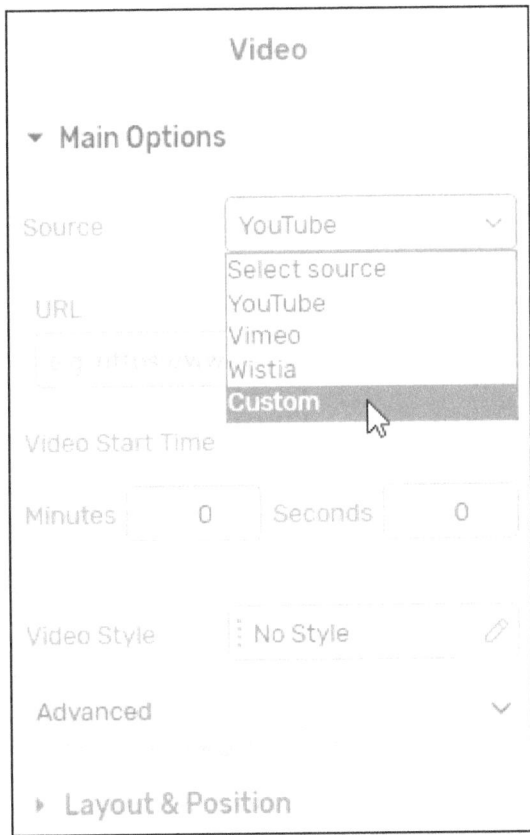

Figure 73: Video Element Options

After selecting the source, choose the video you want to show and move it onto your post or page. To control size and position, move it into a Content Box.

Continue Your Journey

with Thrive

Figure 74: Video Inserted onto Page

You can choose from four different display types. Here the video is being played in the black tablet display.

Figure 75: Playing the Video

Continue Your Journey

with Thrive

WordPress Content

With this element, you can insert content using the standard WordPress classic editor.

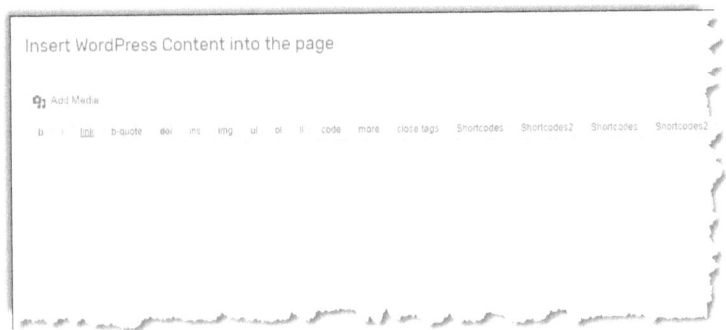

Figure 76: Insert WordPress Content

One application for this is when you are using Thrive Architect to add more content to a page originally created with the WordPress editor.

Call to Action

The Call to Action element allows you to choose from a number of templates that include a button with a link.

Continue Your Journey

with Thrive

Choose Template

Figure 77: Select Call to Action Template

The chosen template is displayed.

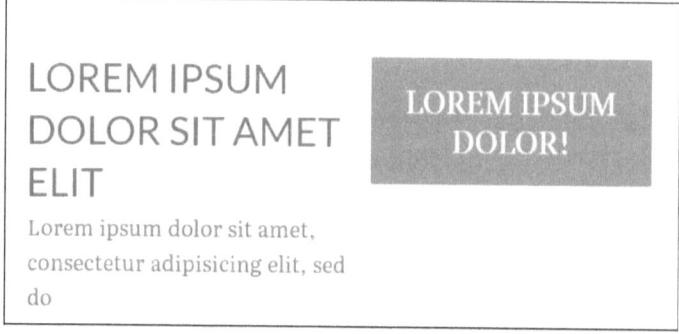

Figure 78: Template Displayed Ready for Tailoring

Modify it with the copy you want and the destination to go to when the button is pressed.

Continue Your Journey

with Thrive

YOU: AN INTERNET
MARKETER IN 9 DAYS!

Download Part 1 of the course FREE

Get Part 1 Now

Figure 79: The Modified Call to Action

The copy, size and color have all been modified and a destination URL added to the button's options.

Contact Form

This element puts a contact form on your page or post so that a visitor can contact you by email.

Figure 80: Contact Form Element

You can control all aspects of the contact form, including the fields that appear on it, its size and appearance, button color, the email address the details are to be sent to and so on.

Continue Your Journey

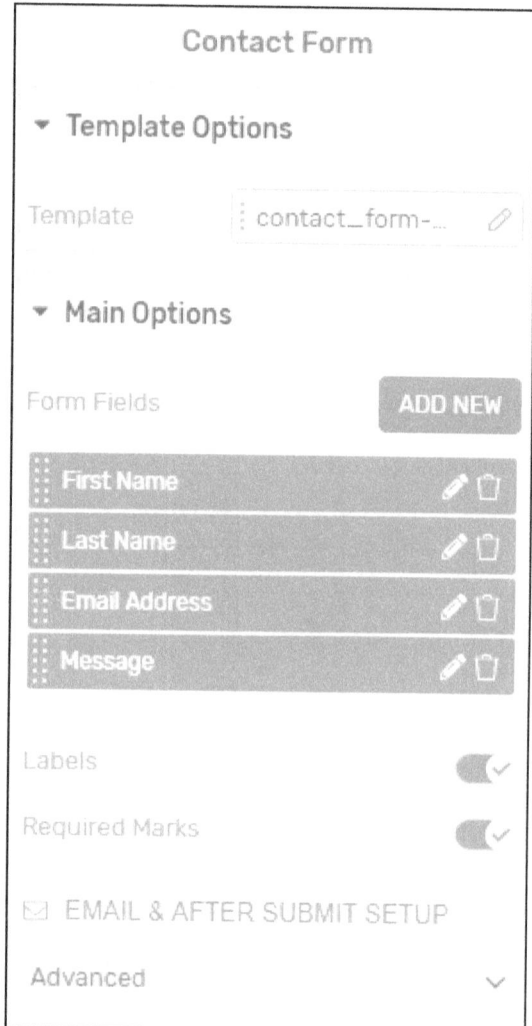

Figure 81: Contact Form Options

Click on *Email & After Submit Setup* to specify what happens
when the button is pressed.

Continue Your Journey

with Thrive

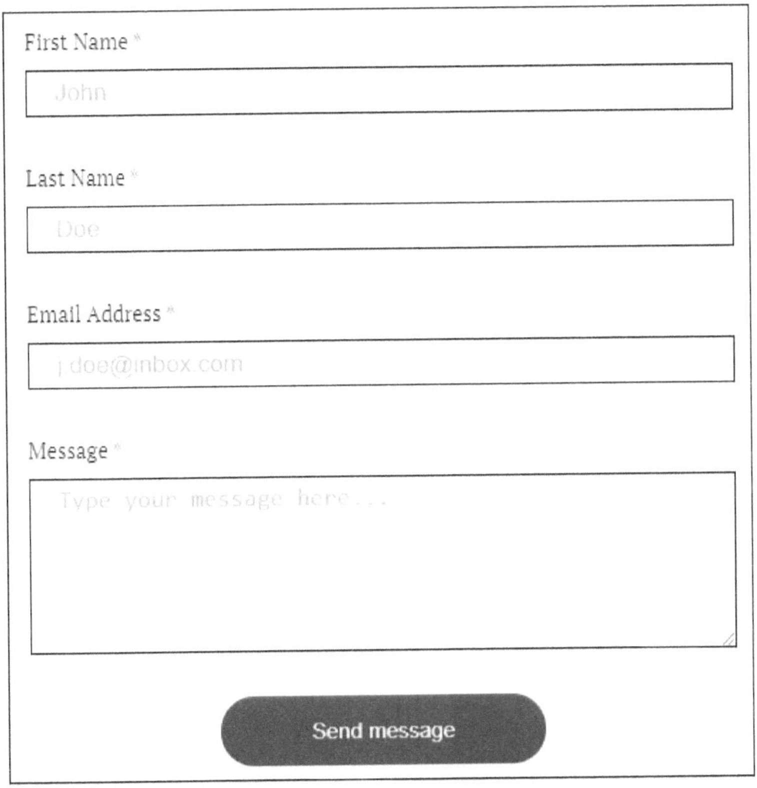

First Name *

> John

Last Name *

> Doe

Email Address *

> j.doe@inbox.com

Message *

> Type your message here...

Send message

Figure 82: Modified Contact Form

Continue Your Journey

with Thrive

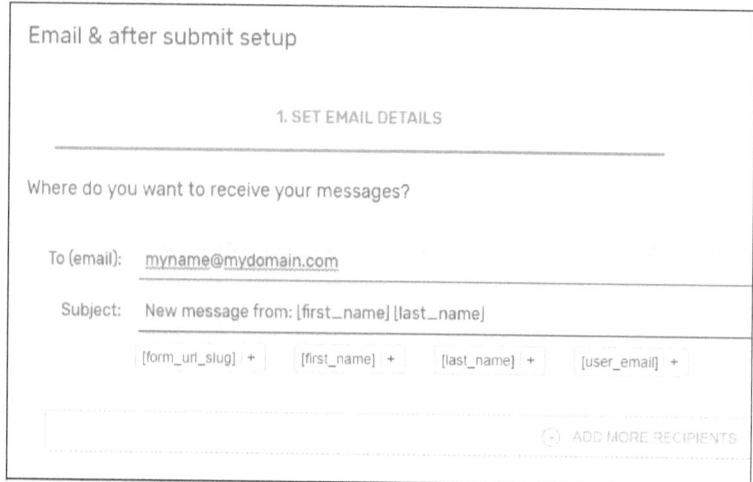

Figure 83: Set Up the Email Details

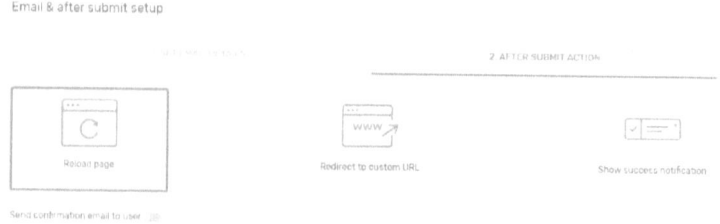

Figure 84: Set Up the After Submit Action

You can choose between reloading the page, redirecting to a custom URL or showing a success notification.

You can also choose to send a confirmation email to your visitor.

Continue Your Journey

with Thrive

Guarantee Box

If you are selling something from your site and want to offer a guarantee, the Guarantee Box element offers a number of different templates to choose from.

Figure 85: Select a Guarantee Template

You can edit every aspect of the template, including copy, color and image. For size and position control, put the template inside a Content Box.

Numbered List

No surprise that the Numbered List element puts a numbered list on the post or page. It's one that you have more control over that the Word type ordered list available from the standard editing toolbar.

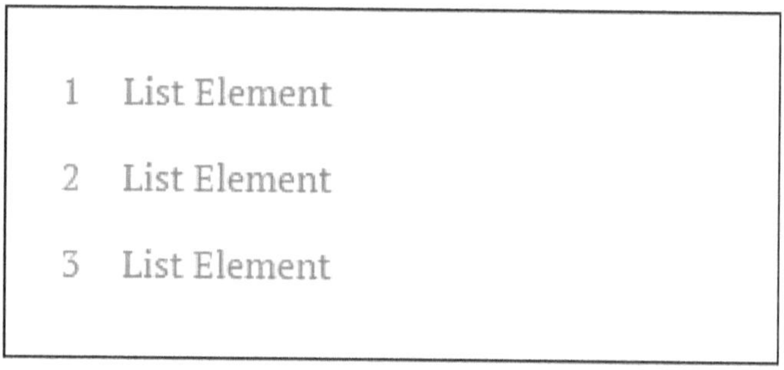

1   List Element

2   List Element

3   List Element

Figure 86: Default Numbered List

You can add more elements and control the font, spacing and so on using the options panel.

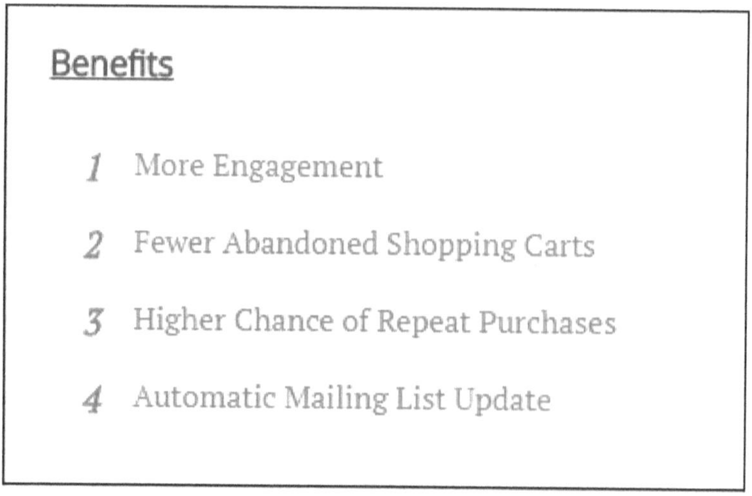

Benefits

1   More Engagement

2   Fewer Abandoned Shopping Carts

3   Higher Chance of Repeat Purchases

4   Automatic Mailing List Update

Figure 87: Modified Numbered List

Continue Your Journey

with Thrive

Pricing Table

The Pricing Table element displays a table comparing the prices of different products or (frequently) multiple versions of the one product.

For example, you might have a membership site that offers Silver, Gold and Platinum memberships with contrasting benefits and prices.

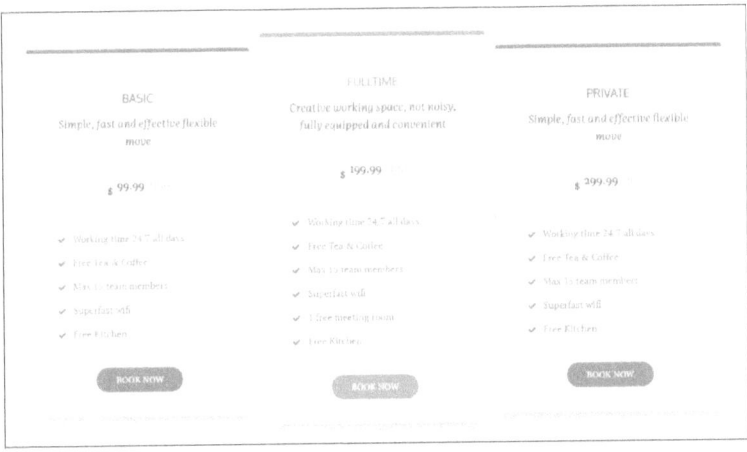

Figure 88: Pricing Table Element

Three columns are shown by default, but you can control this in the Pricing Tables options panel.

You can also change the template be selecting from others available.

Continue Your Journey

with Thrive

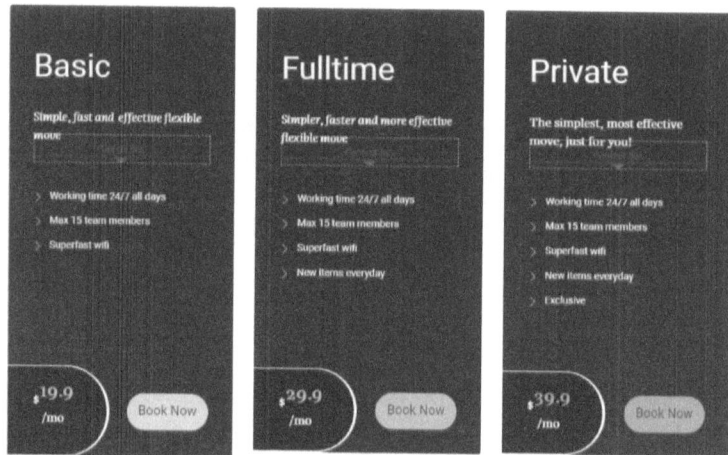

Figure 89: Pricing Table Element New Template

The Pricing Table options panel gives you control over all aspects of the pricing table, including what action to take when a button is pressed.

Continue Your Journey

with Thrive

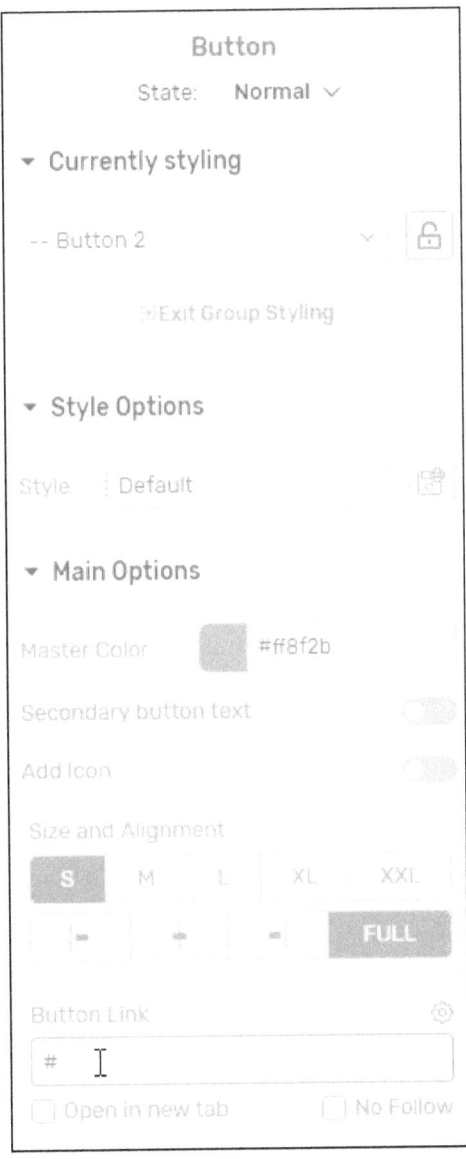

Figure 90: Pricing Table Button Options

Continue Your Journey

with Thrive

Styled Box

The Styled Box element allows you to put text and/or images inside a box styled to stand out in some way. There are many templates to choose from.

Lorem Ipsum Dolor

Lorem ipsum dolor sit amet, consectetur adipisicing elit, sed do eiusmod tempor incididunt ut labore et dolore magna aliqua. Ut enim ad minim veniam, quis nostrud exercitation ullamco laboris nisi ut aliquip ex ea commodo consequat. Duis aute irure dolor in reprehenderit in voluptate velit esse cillum dolore eu fugiat nulla pariatur. Excepteur sint occaecat cupidatat non proident, sunt in culpa qui officia deserunt mollit anim id est laborum.

Figure 91: A Simple Styled Box with Heading and Text

Continue Your Journey

with Thrive

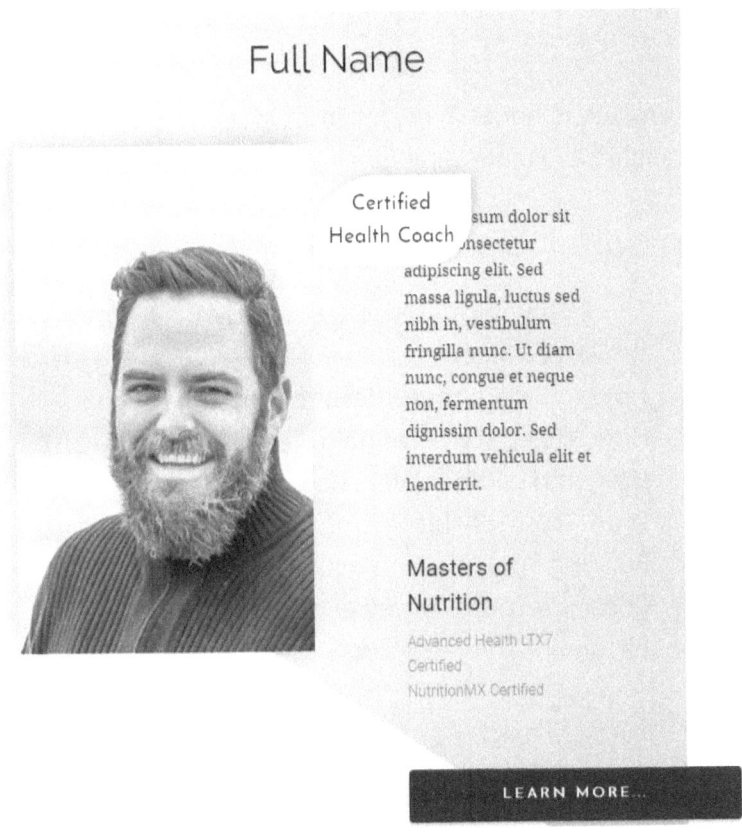

Figure 92: Styled Box Used as a Bio

There are many other templates available.

Continue Your Journey
with Thrive

The Rest of the Books

Here are all the books in my Internet Marketing FAST series, all available as Kindle Singles.

Available Now

1. The 4 Things You Must Know (to Make Money While You Sleep)
2. How to Select Your Internet Marketing Niche
3. How to Register a Domain Name
4. How to Host Your Website
5. WordPress for the Technically Challenged
6. Building Your Website with Thrive
7. Continue Your Journey with Thrive
8. Become a Thrive Expert

Not Yet Available

9. Become an Affiliate Marketing Ninja
10. Become an E-Commerce Ninja
11. The Deadly Combo of Blog Posts and Landing Pages
12. Google is Your New Best Friend
13. Building Your Mailing List
14. All About Free and Paid Traffic
15. How to Publish Your Book on Amazon
16. The Secret to Making Money with Your Internet Businesses (after You've Done Everything Else)

Continue Your Journey

with Thrive

You can get the Kindle and Paperback links to the books on Amazon at

https://superaffiliatechallenge.com/internet-marketing-fast-books-from-amazon/

Continue Your Journey
with Thrive

About the Author

As an 80 year old (in 2024) fitness fanatic and successful internet marketer, Phil Lancaster is a bit of an anomaly.

Through a combination of bad luck and bad business decisions, he found himself broke and alone at 74.

Now, a few years later, he has several internet businesses that combine to bring him a 6-figure income.

It wasn't easy and he got burned a few times on the way, but he reckons that anyone can do it with the right road map.

He wants to help you to get started the way he did, but without making the same mistakes.

Anyone, from student to baby boomer (and older) can make money through the internet.

Phil's IM Fast series of mini-books will get you started. At just $2.99 each, you won't find a better investment.

www.ingramcontent.com/pod-product-compliance
Lightning Source LLC
Chambersburg PA
CBHW020603220526

45463CB00006B/2433